Poems, Prayers, and Praises

From the Broken to the Broken

Brenda Lineberger

ISBN 979-8-88832-301-4 (paperback)
ISBN 979-8-88832-302-1 (digital)

Copyright © 2023 by Brenda Lineberger

All rights reserved. No part of this publication may be reproduced, distributed, or transmitted in any form or by any means, including photocopying, recording, or other electronic or mechanical methods without the prior written permission of the publisher. For permission requests, solicit the publisher via the address below.

Christian Faith Publishing
832 Park Avenue
Meadville, PA 16335
www.christianfaithpublishing.com

Printed in the United States of America

This is a prayer for a family losing their sister, mother, or daughter to cancer.

It's so hard to say goodbye, and you feel so helpless and don't know what to say or do, but being beside them and holding their hand is the most loving thing one can ever do.

Walking Each Other Home

O Father, with sadness, fear, and tear-stained faces, they turn to You and ask, "Why now, Lord? Why so soon? Why this way? They need Your grace, Lord, they need grace. Breathe peace, courage, and strength into each heart as they surround her with the love of a precious family, and they take her by the hand to walk their daughter, sister, wife, and mother home to You. That's what family does; they walk each other home and whisper a picture so they can see the smile on their daddy's face when he sees his little girl running into his embrace. The stories they

have to share will take an eternity in
that holy place.

This is my prayer in the name of Jesus Christ.

Bradford Haupt was a sweet, God-loving man I met in a small life group / Bible study.

He spent twenty-four years in a wheelchair because of a horrible motorcycle accident, but even though he suffered constant pain, his faith and spirit was so evident that there is no telling how many lives he touched. He certainly touched mine.

I wrote this for him. We lost him in the family, but heaven received him.

A Letter to Brad

Oh, Brad,
Sad hearts left behind to cry
A Christ-filled spirit
Lifted by God's own angels beyond
    the sky
Into the arms of Jesus and your baby
    girl
With all the others
At the gates of pearl
So patiently they waited to see you
    again
But you were needed here
To lend Jesus a hand

So with your wheels of metal, you
          laid out the rows
And planted seeds of faith
Leaving behind you a garden of souls
          for Jesus to save

Dear Brad,

You will not be forgotten, for
your life glorified Christ, and your
great big heart so loved our God.
Our lives were made richer to
just witness your faith. So your silly
grin, love of history, guns and gad-
gets, and devotion to your beloved
family and friends will bring smiles
to our faces and joy to our hearts.
See you on the other side!

Between the Manger and the Cross

The seed of hope planted in prophecy took His first breath on that first Christmas Day

A divine promise in a manger He lay

An obedient father and a virgin mother gaze on their baby

Their Messiah, their Savior, and they knew what God had sent Him to do

He came to teach, heal, serve, save, and do His Father's will

He met scorn, rejection, betrayal, and finally death on a hill

The earth shook, walls came down, veils torn, and the gates of heaven opened

Two trees planted long ago, one became a manger, one became a cross

Both held our Savior, and both held eternal life for us all

Between the manger and the cross

One Three-Letter Word

Jesus knew the cost
He planted the tree that would be His cross
God placed Himself as Jesus Christ on that cross
His life wasn't taken, He gave it
There was blood, sweat, tears, agony, wrath
Earthquakes, darkness, thunder, forgiveness, promise, death, and resurrection
All given in exchange for one "three-letter word"
Yes
Yes, I choose You, Lord
Yes, I believe You died for my sins
Yes, I will follow You
Yes, I will praise You
Yes, I am Yours, and yes, You are mine
One three-letter word

A Sweet Rescue

I saw one of the sweetest acts of care, compassion, and rescue, and it touched me so deep in my heart that I just couldn't get it out of my mind.

I was driving along, asking God to guard my heart against something I was concerned about when I saw a man step into the middle of the road and put his hand up to stop me. Then he gently bent down and tenderly cupped a tiny bird into the palms of his hands and drew it up to his chest. He looked into his hands, and on his face, I saw love. I asked him if the bird was okay, and he said he thought it had a broken beak and some larger birds were chasing it. He had to save it.

I just couldn't stop thinking about it, and finally, I think I got it. That's a picture of our Father gently bending down, scooping his hurt, broken, scared children up, pulling us to His heart and holding us. No safer place could we ever be. Our hearts beat next to His, healing as He holds us close.

Changed

He reached down from on high and took hold
of me; he drew me out of deep waters.

He rescued me from my powerful enemy,
from my foes, who were too strong for me.

—2 Samuel 22:17–18

Jesus, You have walked with me through the fire, hurt, brokenness, and despair, and I am so blessed that You are walking with me tonight and allowing me to honor first Your sacrifice on the cross, honor the blood You shed for me, honor Your love for me, and finally Your rescue from my enemy.

I leave behind sin, shame, regret, and all the handiwork of my enemy. My heart is now a holy place filled with joy, hope, fearlessness, and praise, and Satan is not welcome.

My Christmas Prayer Today

Holy Father, Holy Jesus, Holy Spirit.

Lord, sometimes Christmas can be difficult because of loss, regret, aloneness, so today I ask You to, in Your everlasting love and mercy, equip us with the faith, the strength, and the wisdom to overcome those thoughts and feelings and replace them with hope, trust, patience, and understanding and include the joy, the good news, the light that You are and the thankfulness that because You were born to us, You came down here to us, that the answer to this prayer is not only a possibility but a promise (John 15:7).

Amen.

Wait on the Lord: be of good courage, and he shall
strengthen thine heart: wait, I say, on the Lord.

—Psalm 27:14

Call unto me, and I will answer thee, and show thee
great and mighty things, which thou knowest not.

—Jeremiah 33:3

The Answer

Revival = the great and mighty things
His story told simply as it is true
Using the broken and redeemed to tell us who it was
Born to die for me and you
The enemy, so clever, using his all
To distract the hurting from hearing God's call
But *this* story of redemption and salvation
Not confined to the binding of a book but is bigger,
        thunderous, loud
Deeper than the seas, brighter than the sun
And able to pierce the hardest heart.

This story, *His* story, *is* the answer to revival prayers
This story is *revival*
Blessed to be even a spec in the atmosphere
Of that much holiness in one place
Made me know what I see *is His face*.

Embrace the never-changing, power-filled story
And give to Him who lived it *all the glory*.

Hope Has Risen

Today hope rose from the dead. Today you rose Jesus. Today hope rose for us too. Hope that we, too, could go home to our Father. You and You alone gave us the gift no one else could ever give. You gave us hope, a destination, a reason to live, and a reason to believe in something bigger than we are—hope that is alive.

A hope that grows, spills over, and spreads. This hope changes lives, changes eternities, defeats death, feeds the hungry, restores, and revives. You cannot find this hope any place but one. Jesus Christ is the only hope. Hope rose thousands of years ago. Jesus is the one hope that is alive, solid as a rock, pure as a diamond, and larger than the galaxies, and the access is a simple prayer. Once hope embraces you, He will never let you go.

Hope rose today.

The Account of My Salvation

I was walking along a path when I saw a bridge across a body of dark, murky water. Close behind me walks a man; I did not know him. He was silent, and I couldn't see his face.

I said to him, "I think there's someone in the water."

I could only see a glimpse of someone in the water and was afraid they had already drowned. There was no movement. For a second, I thought I had jumped in to help; I was wet but still standing on the bridge. Then I saw the stranger dive in, and he disappeared into the water. In the very next instant, I was standing off the bridge on solid ground next to the stranger. Something was different; there was so much light, and I couldn't see anything but his silhouette, just the shape of a person. I couldn't see his face. Off to my right, I saw a crowd of similar shapes and heard celebrating. I don't know if it was songs or shouts, but it sounded happy. I was so confused, not scared, but confused.

Then, I woke up. Yes, it was a dream. I relived the entire dream for days, trying to sort it out. I had so many ideas about who was in the water, who the stranger was, and why I couldn't see faces.

Then one sweet morning, He told me.

Jesus Christ was the man following me; I was the person drowning. He continues to this very day to explain the details of my salvation. That dream has never faded, and I go back to it every day.

You see, I was so broken and had no hope, no light, and nothing to hold on to, and I wanted death to take me so the hurt would stop. I believed that would be the only way. But He had other plans.

My salvation story.

Choices Made Crosses Built
One, Two, Three

Three crosses
Two thieves
One Savior
Two were guilty
One was innocent
Two were placed on a cross
One placed Himself on a cross
One prayed
Two mocked
One heart repented
One mocked still
One chose Christ
One did not
One is with Christ today
One is not

Time, Precious Time

Don't put off till tomorrow
What can you do today?
It could change everything!
Lord, ignite a fire in my heart to not give my time
    away to the world
But to a life lived to give to You honor and praise
    and glory
Seasoned with the salt of wisdom, courage, and set
    apart
Faith-filled and anointed as You write my story
And make it all count
Time to build the church
Time to encourage and to be the light
Time to serve, and time to plant good seeds into
    good soil
Time to see a harvest of saved souls
Awaken in me, Lord, the sleeping purpose gifted to
    me to glorify You and Your goodness
May each day begin and end in pursuit of the prize of
    Your upward call through Jesus Christ
No time to waste
Today is yesterday's tomorrow!

Red Letters

A journey begins when to Christ, our hearts we give
Faith enters and a new way to live
Not easy, this path of light
Testing starts early, and we must learn to fight
The enemy is real, his identity, he hides
In things appearing innocent until we look inside
Reject confusion, fear, or things of the world
Don't settle for less than the treasures of the Lord
From the enemy, the *red letters* will set you free
Remind the enemy, "It is written," he will have to flee
Red letters, bold and true
And against them, there's nothing Satan can do
Precious and priceless, the voice of Christ
His holy words written in red, as is the blood of His
    sacrifice

Praying through Psalm 23

Lord, come, be my shepherd. I want no other. Show me again the green pastures and the still waters. Restore my weary soul. Hold my hand and lead me in paths of righteousness for Your name's sake. Though I walk through the valleys in shadows of hurt, disappointments, and even death, I will fear no evil, for You are with me to protect and comfort me. Surely goodness and mercy will follow me to the home You have prepared for me, and I shall dwell in Your house forever and ever.

Amen.

Words, Tender and Sweet

Whispers a king
A soul to keep
A lamb's heart so beloved
A divine shepherd
Come from above
To show the way
That leads to home and to hear Him say,
"You're safe now, never alone."

Broken

O God, my heart cries out
It's breaking again
You know what it's about
Come near, just as You said You would
Tell me again, You'll work it for good
Bring comfort and calm and whisper, "You're mine"
For in Your presence, peace, I'll find
In You, I trust, and in Jesus's name, I pray

Open Windows and Open Doors

My hunger is great
Lord, let it be
Let me grow still, closer to Thee

Remove any clutter between my heart and Yours
Open the windows and all the doors
No shade or shadows
Where sin could hide
Only light, holy light inside

Let my soul run free, dance, and play
Grow and learn and praise and pray
In the light between my heart and Yours
With open windows and open doors

Remember the Cross

Light from the *cross* is cast.
Cutting through sin and salvation.
Dividing future from past.
As drops of life fall without sound, mixed with a
    mother's tears on now holy ground.
And as hate surrounded the *cross* and angels held
    their breath,
He prayed, "Forgive them that no souls be lost."
They knew not then that they were redeemed by the
    blood on their hands.
"It is finished," He gasped and lowered His thorn-
    crowned head and breathed His last.
In the hands of God, His Spirit at rest, and His crim-
    son-streaked body laid in a tomb.
But a grave could not hold Him, death was defeated.
Victory belongs to Christ, our Savior.
Remember the *cross*, remember the *cost*.

John 10:17–18
Matthew 20:28

He Waits

"Please do not go away until I come back and bring my offering and set it before You. And the Lord said, 'I will wait until you return'" (Judges 6:18). Oh, how this spoke to me!

And He waits
He waited for Joseph to learn skills for a nation to feed
He waited for Moses to accept the assignment, a nation to lead
He waited for Elijah, who had fears to face
He waited for Esther to pray for courage, where she was placed
He waited for David to confess and ask for grace
He waited for Jonah to obey and do His will
He waited for Thomas to see His scars that he could put his doubts to rest
He waited for Peter to fully surrender and become the man Jesus knew he could be
He waited for Paul in a road and took his sight so he could see

And He waits
Life is but a whisper of time
Don't leave Him waiting
He's waiting to tell us, "You are mine."

The Gift

On wind and flame, our friend arrived
The Holy Spirit of God, His name
The third of three of one came to carry on that which
      Christ had begun
A counselor, a shepherd, and a friend to live in each
      heart
Until our days are at end
And on that Pentecost day,
By the power of the Holy Spirit, Peter, the rock, had
      something to say
With unleashed passion, he spoke the gospel, truth
      gave birth to the Church
And her cries were heard around the world
God's gifts have no equal, the virgin birth, the cross,
      the resurrection
And the day of Pentecost and that of the indwelling
      of the Holy Spirit
And on that day, the gift of *His forever presence* in our
      hearts

Live in His Word Equals Live in His Will

God, the Father, author of the living word
He knew, left on our own,
We would surely lose our way home
So with love unmeasurable, big and bold
He made a way, their stories must to be told
He spoke all of creation into existence
Before the written word, He spoke through a burn-
     ing bush,
A mountain, fire, clouds, and even a donkey
Oh, hear His voice now echoing through
His prophets, saints, and sinners
Their footprints cast a path in their wilderness to
     lead us through *our* wilderness
To *our* promised land
Love letters written in the blood of Christ, God's
     own Son
The light, the way, the savior, and the one
The past, present, and the future
Is between these chapters and verses
It's their story, and it's our story

In the beginning, God created the heaven and the earth. (Genesis 1:1)

The grace of our Lord Jesus Christ be with you all. (Revelation 22:21)

Great passion, great love, great mercy, forgiveness, and great grace
A manger, a cross, and an empty grave
Oh, hear His voice now

Open My Eyes to See

Jesus in my Christmas tree

As I gaze upon this tree, show me, Lord, what You
want me to see

The angels, the stars, and the colors all tell the story
of Christ Jesus and His glory

An angel gave Mary the news that she would give
birth to our savior, the Son of God

Green is life and pastures, He leads us to rest

Purple, His royalty, a king no less

Gold paves the streets of heaven

Silver, the price for His life

The tree became a cross

Red, His blood, His sacrifice

White, His holiness

The angels returned to announce His birth to shep-
herds and wise men, and a star marked the place

I see it now, Lord, I see Christ Jesus in my Christmas
tree

Pieces of Heaven

A glimpse into glory, a peek at the wonder of wonders
Way above where eagles fly beyond the stars and
    beyond the sky
The Holy Spirit gives us eyes to see
The pieces of heaven to you and me
We see thrones, crowns, angels, and saints clothed
    in white
Streets of pure, clear gold, gardens, and the tree of life
Twelve precious stones, pristine and flawless, are the
    walls
And twelve gates of pearl will open to those who heed
    His call
Inside there's no sickness, no death
Bodies are made new, no more vessels of clay
As the hand of God wipes our tears away
Peace and joy when we finally see this place
And the pieces of heaven reveal to us His face

1 Corinthians 2:9–10
Revelations 21:19–21
Matthew 11:25

Birthdays

Birthdays come in three
First, we are born of the union of the Creator and
the created
First breaths taken, each of us was meant to be
After years of searching for meaning, we find a God-
shaped void inside our heart
So with bowed head and bended knee, born now
into the family of God
With Christ, His Son alive in our souls, one day, we
hear the upward call
And are born again through the gates of heaven, a
new body and a new home
Three birthdays
One, we had no choice
Second, we had to choose
Next, we were chosen

> Except a man be born again,
> he cannot see the kingdom of God.
> (John 3:3)

You were chosen by God the Father long ago. He knew you were to become His children Happy Birthday times three! (1 Peter 1:2–4)

Pages of My Story

Lord, my story recorded in Your book, a blank page
      before me each day
With pen in hand, what do I want my story to say?
As You open the book to read it to the angels and to
      me
This is what I want You to see.

Oh, this was a difficult day
Broken, her heart lay in pieces
I scooped them up with My hand
Held them close to My heart, and the healing began
And on this day, everything was changed
Her soul was saved, no longer lost
My Son came and led her to the cross
And this was a special day too, as water washed over
      her and with a silent shout
to the world, in the name of the Father, the Son, and
      the Holy Spirit, she heard
a whisper, "You're Mine."

This day, my favorite day, the day the angels brought
      her home to Me.
I counted the days and longed to see her face-to-face.

Oh, my Father, just to hear Your voice reading the
words of my story and with a smile
Tell me that I won the prize of Your upward call
through Jesus Christ
This is my prayer: Philippians 3:14.
Thank You, Jesus, for taking the sins out of my story
and nailing them to the cross.

Amen.

We are the authors of our stories.
Psalm 56:8
Psalm 138:16
Daniel 7:10

Gethsemane

A heart so heavily filled with fear and dread
His holy face to the ground, pleading for mercy
But surrenders His will to the Father's instead
Christ knew from the beginning, planned at length
Of the betrayal, the beating, the cross, even the nails
But the love of the Father was His strength
Knowing death He would face, and the Father would
    forsake
He became the sacrifice, the pure, perfect lamb of
    God
Then took His final steps to Calvary to give His life
    for ours
Only the royal blood from the King of kings, the
    Lord of lords
Could redeem all generations past, present, future,
    even to the end of age
For our Savior would not die the death of a saint but
    that of a sinner
And the measure of His love was the distance from
    the arms of
The Father to a cross on a hill

About the Author

Brenda Lineberger lives in the town of Mooresville, North Carolina, near Charlotte. She enjoys gardening and spending time with her two grown children and grandkids. She lives with a sweet Great Dane named Zeus, also called a country gentleman, and a somewhat grumpy little green parrot named Scooby. She writes these little poems, prayers, and praises in hopes that one who has been rescued can help one that needs rescuing.

www.ingramcontent.com/pod-product-compliance
Lightning Source LLC
Chambersburg PA
CBHW022038150726
47990CB00004B/1521